Handle With Stardust And Daydreams

Pooja Gupta

BookLeaf Publishing

India | USA | UK

Made with ❤ on the BookLeaf Publishing Platform
www.bookleafpub.in
www.bookleafpub.com

Dedication

For Mumma, who thought hiding my novels would make me study more, and Papa, who ensured I never ran out of books to get lost in!

Preface

This little book is made of stardust, daydreams, and a generous scoop of overthinking.
It holds poems written on sleepy nights, in crowded cafes, during bus rides, and sometimes while pretending to listen during serious conversations. These are thoughts that refused to stay quiet—some soft, some silly, all a little sparkly.
If you've ever cried over cartoons, believed your coffee could fix your soul, or felt like a walking contradiction— this is for you.
Please handle with care. And maybe a hot chocolate.

Acknowledgements

To the books I've read under blankets, behind textbooks, during train rides, and in quiet corners—you raised me. Every story, every scribbled margin note, every tear-stained page added something to this heart. You made me believe in the power of words.

To the authors who taught me how to feel deeply and write freely—thank you for showing me that softness is strength.

To BookLeaf Publishing, thank you for opening a door and smiling when I walked through it with all my messy, magical thoughts.

To the people who never made me feel too much or too little—you know who you are. Your kindness grew roots in my words.

And lastly, to the version of me who out of blue actually started typing—thank you.

1. Fairytales and Burnt Toast

For now, I am trusting the process,
A humorous little Insta-worthy thought though—
Does the process know I'm trusting it?
What's meant for me will come back,
Disguised as new opportunities,
Or maybe second chances.
Maybe as a long-lost hobby,
Or a sudden streak of luck?
Maybe as the fruit of patience,
Or the Cosmic Dance of Karma?
Maybe in the form of blessings,
Or as proof of The Burnt Toast Theory?
But time is slipping like sand,
And my patience is so low,
It probably needs a caffeine fix.
Does manifestation work?
Or those daily temple visits—
Like, a sure shot?

I mean, I can work hard, sure,For now, I am trusting the
process,
But why does my mind treat "what I want?"
Like a riddle, playing hard to get?
For now, do I grind every day?
Or do I just take off and rebel?
I want to travel—should I just go?
Is 27 the perfect age to be reckless?
Should I secretly use my vacation days,
Instead of hoarding them like a responsible adult?
Maybe, just maybe, this is my plot twist,
The chapter before the magic kicks in.
Like a lost slipper waiting to be found,
Or a beanstalk that hasn't sprouted yet.
In the end, the story always unfolds,
And somehow, it all turns out just right—
At least, that's what the fairytales say.
And if life is a fairytale in the making,
Well, my mirror says I'm pretty enough to be in one.

2. Happy?

In class 4th, my favorite teacher asked us to write an
essay on **"The Happiest Day of My Life."**

Is it not enough to be happy?

But what is happiness?

Is it the fuzzy feeling I get when the boy I like says I look
pretty?
Or the buzzy feeling I get when I go to the mountains?
Or the excitement of being in a bookstore?
Or the comforting feeling of being teased by my friends?
Or the warmth of going back home?
Or the flow of endless talks with my favorite cousin?
Or the peaceful feeling of reading a book in a pretty
coffee shop?
Or the eureka moment when I crack a code I thought I
never would?
Or the surprise of getting a birthday gift?

Or the peace of seeing a sky full of stars after countless
years?
Or the fluffy feeling of spotting candy cotton clouds?

Maybe it's all?

But the thing is,
What if I want to be happy always?
What if I don't want the happiest day to be just one day?
What if I want the happiest life?

3. The Poetry of Being Me

You know the little things?
The ones people wonder why I'm so obsessed with?
Like the cups of coffee I go through—
Sometimes instant,
Sometimes in a pretty little café,
Like tiny rituals of comfort.
Why do I hoard so many books?
"When do you even find the time to read them?"
Is that even your business?
Or why I like pink,
Why I adore all things soft and silly?
Is there a rule that says my likes must grow up with me?
I *want* my world to be whimsical.
I *want* my room, my clothes, my accessories—
To look like they belong to an eight-year-old's dream.
So what?
Yes, I need chocolate every day.
So what?
Yes, I trust too quickly—
Kindness makes me believe.

So what?
Do I need permission to love anime and rom-coms?
To admire artists who feel too much?
To paint without reason?
To sometimes just be alone,
Because that's when I breathe easiest?
Have you ever seen my diary?
The tear stains, the crossed-out words,
The quiet wars I fight on paper?
Do I really need to justify the things
That keep me standing?
Yes, I sleep with a soft toy.
Yes, I still dream like a child.
Yes, I crave peace more than anything.
So what?
Have you seen the scars on my wrist?
Do you know the silence from those I trusted most?
You don't.
So why would you question
The things that make me feel safe?
Let me have my little coffee.
Let me read in corners.
Let me wear what makes me feel soft.
Let me hope, travel, create, heal.
Let me—
Please, let me be.
Even if you don't understand.

Even if the world never claps.
Let me be soft,
Please—let me be free.
Even just a little.

4. The little boy in Shantikunj

In the land of ashrams and Rudraksha trees,
I met a boy, no more than eight,
His shirt neatly tucked—perhaps his school uniform,
His brown eyes shimmered with dreams and hope.
I stopped for the mixed sprouts he was selling,
And asked, casually, "Do you go to school?"
He nodded, then added softly,
"I do, but today I must stand in for my father—
His leg is fractured, and someone has to work."
And just like that, the conversation was no longer casual.
With quiet resolve, he spoke of duty and dreams.
Of burdens far too heavy for his tender years.
I thought of my life—so much lighter,
And yet, how often had I stumbled under its weight?
Even now, when life tightens its grip,
That boy walks into my mind,
Still selling, still standing, still carrying.
And I let him remind me
What strength looks like.

By now, he must be a teenager,
His school shirt still tucked in, maybe.
His brown eyes still burning—
With dreams, with hope, with something heavier
That never left.

5. Namjooning

Somewhere quiet, somewhere mine,
Where time moves slow, where the world unwinds.
A small wooden cottage tucked between trees,
Remember the hut with seven miner dwarfs?
Yeah, that— but with a coffee machine.
The library from *Beauty and the Beast,*
Red berries, yellow sunflowers grinning,
Birds that won't shut up, butterflies too impatient to sit
still.
A little farther, a pond—
Somehow filtered, somehow drinkable,
Even with croaking frogs and lazy ducks floating
around.
A bean bag—mine, sanitized, soft as clouds,
Wrapped in baby pink, waiting under a cherry tree,
With a portable fan—because, well, you never know.
Maybe a talking German Shepherd?
I mean, who wouldn't want a built-in hype man?
A shelf inside a tree trunk,
Packed with paint, brushes, books—

Everything I need, right there.

And is it *too much* to ask for food delivery service?

6. Between Pages and People

My father once said,
"Books are your best friends—they never leave you."
True.
They sat beside me when I was sad,
Took me to places I never meant to visit,
Gave me peace when I was restless,
Led me through the world's best and worst emotions.
Some stayed.
Some I had to let go—for my own good.
But then,
I found others who never left.
I got him—who never gave up on me.
I got Mumma—who never stopped praying.
I got my aunts—more like big sisters than anything else.
I got my little cousin—who calls me his best friend.
I got people I call brothers—not by blood,
But because they solve my mess and protect my peace.
I got childhood friends who watched me shift
From sunshine to shadow and stayed anyway.

I got friends who can't picture me sad,
Mentors who wish me only light.
If I keep listing,
This list might never end.
So why do I still feel alone sometimes?
Why does my mind keep playing tricks on me?
Who taught it these games?
Why do humans feel everything all at once?
Why can't I just be grateful and let go?
Why must I turn it into poetry just to understand
myself?
Maybe this is how I breathe.
Maybe this is how I remember.
Maybe poetry is the only language
That speaks when nothing else does.
Maybe I'm not alone.
Just learning how to listen.

.

7. Ephemeral

Have you ever seen cherry blossoms?
I have not.
I wonder if they are just baby pink,
or if they hold secret shades—
dusky rose, blushing dawn,
Maybe the color of love letters left unread.

Do they smell sweet, like strawberries in spring?
Like vanilla cake, warm and soft?
Or do they carry something wilder, deeper,
A scent that lingers like a half-remembered dream?
Or maybe—maybe they have no scent at all
because beauty like that needs no proof.

Are they precious because they slip away too soon?
Because the wind steals them before we are ready,
because they teach us that nothing truly stays?
Is that why they stand for fortune and revival—
because we all long for another chance,
another bloom, another breath?

I wonder—
Would we still call them beautiful if they were brown or
black?
Would they still be poetry if they weren't soft and pale?
But then again, maybe beauty isn't meant to be reasoned
with.
Maybe cherry blossoms are just cherry blossoms.
And that is enough.

8. 27

I read somewhere,
As we grow, our experiences, our emotions,
Stretch out like wild branches on an old tree.
27—the perfect age.
The weirdest, messiest, funniest.
Deadlines choking—work, life, everything in between.
Reminders everywhere—how I *should* have settled by
now.
A great career, a perfect family, flawless health...
Not an inch less than *great!*
But honestly? I don't *feel* any different.
It's just that everyone around me won't shut up about it.
Too young for some,
Too old for others.
I have friends I'd trust with my life,
And strangers I once trusted with all my heart.
Dozens of things I ache to do,
Hundreds of things I can't stand.
Still light up like a kid over some things,
And roll my eyes like an old woman over most.

I'm closer to my papa,
Best friends with mumma now.
I get my rebellious, annoying teenage brother *a little*
more,
And I love my little cousin more than anything.
Not ashamed of therapy.
Not hating early nights.
Can buy as many damn books as I want.
Cutting toxic people? Easier.
Saying *sorry* for the right ones? Easier too.
I doubt myself a little less.
Love myself a lot more.
I see my responsibilities now,
And my grandfather's stories hit different.
When I lay it out like this—
27 doesn't seem too bad.
A little grown-up, a little kid.

9. Summer That Stayed

Summer smelled like dust and mangoes,
Like scraped knees and laughter that never ran out.
With my favorite cousin by my side,
We ran wild under the scorching sun,
Played kho kho till the sky turned orange,
Dirt in our hair, sweat on our backs,
Hearts full of nothing but the game.
Ten rupees in our tiny fists,
Standing at the shop, whispering plans—
Candy? Ice lollies? Chips?
So serious, like we were making history.
In the backyard, our hands sank into warm, wet earth,
Rolling, shaping, building—tiny pots, crooked toys,
Fingers caked in mud, hearts swelling with pride.
Afternoons were for making up stories,
Talking in hushed voices, planning every scene.
Then we played them out like they were real,
Living in the worlds we created.
Matching clothes, secret codewords,
Fights that felt like the end of the world,

And make-ups that came just as fast.
Passing scribbled chits between us,
Side by side, laughing without a word.
Rushing home for our favorite cartoons,
Our fixed two-hour Saturday TV ritual.
Buying pirated CDs with saved-up change,
As if we owned a piece of something forbidden.
Mangoes dripped down our hands,
Sticky, sweet, endless.
The lights would go, and the game began—
Hiding in shadows, breath held tight,
Waiting to be found, hoping not to be.
Now the streets feel wider, the laughter echoes softer.
No matching clothes, no ten-rupee debates,
No backyard clay toys or scribbled chits.
Just memories that feel like sun-warmed skin.
Bittersweet, like mangoes at season's end.

10. Beyond the Verdicts

Why do they judge so easily?
Must I always defend my say?
Do I seem too immature, too irresponsible—
Careless, unreliable—in their eyes?
I understand their reasoning;
I see their expectations.
But for once—just once—could someone
Offer trust in return?
I hold the potential to craft my own life,
Yet I question: does it truly matter?
Sometimes it does, and sometimes it does not.
My choices form my own constellations,
A universe guided only by my inner light.
I now accept that expectations
Often stray from the human heart—
The child within me knows
That life is not bound by others' designs.
So I choose to trust myself,
To keep my head high despite rejection,
To be kind and joyful

Regardless of what happens outside.
In that quiet resolve, my heart grows calm,
And I finally understand:
Happiness isn't a mystery to be solved,
But a journey of living authentically—
A radiant code, uniquely mine.

11. The Weight of Why

Someone once said,
"When people return after leaving once,
It's just their memories you're fond of."
Is that true?
Even if it is—
Isn't life too short to close the doors?
Can't we leave the gates open?
Why must something that made me stronger
Be looked back on with grudge and guilt?
Maybe I wasn't meant to follow their advice.
Maybe this was my potential.
Maybe this was necessary.
Why does everything have to be logically clear?
Why can't we trust the things we can't explain?
Why does everyone keep telling me—
"Be ready for the worst."
Why?
Why do we put so much faith in the negative?
Why are we constantly stuck there?
Why is being optimistic, being trusting—

Seen as immaturity?
If trusting is naïve, then let me be naïve.
If hope is foolish, then let me be a fool.
For I refuse to live in a world
Where fear decides my path.

12. Becoming

**What is this pang of sadness
that visits me time and again?**
Is it the weight of unfulfilled dreams,
or the silent fear of what's to come?
Perhaps it's the ache of severed ties,
ghosts of voices now gone numb.
Maybe it's the fear of abandonment,
or the bitter truth I fail to see—
that I have always been the first
to turn my back on me.
Is it the quiet realization
that I walk this path alone,
searching for solace in echoes,
in a world I've never truly known?
But even the night must bow to dawn,
and wounds will heal with time and grace.
I am not lost, I am becoming—
learning to stand, to hope, to embrace.

13. Whispers I never Chose!

If you're so damn good at doubting,
why don't you doubt the voices in your head
that tear you down every time you try to stand?
The ones that say *you can't.*
The ones that scoff when you even think about wanting
more.
Why don't you doubt the fear that creeps in,
the one that whispers *you'll never make it,*
that laughs in your face when you dream too big—
Fuji? The Northern Lights?
Please.
Not for you. Never for you.
Why don't you question the stories you've sewn,
the threads woven tight, that bind you alone?
Why do you trust the voice that says love is a battlefield
but not the quiet one that says *you deserve it?*
Why do their words weigh more than your truth?
Why do you believe them when they say *you're*
nothing?
Why does your self-worth crumble so easily,

like it was never meant to stand tall?
Why do you never question the screaming, relentless
voice
that swears you are unloved, unseen, unwanted?
Why, in those moments, are you so sure?

Maybe it's time to just listen—
not to them, but to something softer,
something that doesn't bruise when it speaks.
Maybe it's time to wonder—
What if they're wrong?
What if you are more than they'll ever let you believe?
What if—just once—you don't listen?

14. Echoes of the Bell

I remember my school campus, shaded by neem trees,
A little basketball court standing quietly on the side.
I remember the three cream-red buildings,
Their walls echoing laughter, lessons, and time.
I remember the drumbeats and choir at morning
assembly,
The water tank near the stage, still standing still.
Five rupees fine for not speaking English,
A small price for childhood rebellion.
Independence Day parades, the house captains fierce,
Voices rising, flags waving, feet marching in rhythm.
Our turn to conduct assembly—practicing speeches,
Striving to be the best, to be noticed, to belong.
I remember the passage from the graveyard to the
cathedral,
Footsteps hushed, stories whispering through the
stones.
Captain's oath ceremony—right hand raised,
A fleeting moment of power, of promise.
I remember my classroom,

And eighty-four friends who made it feel like home.
Teachers who weren't just teachers,
But pillars, guiding hands, and quiet support.
Activity Saturdays—excitement crackling in the air,
Field trips that felt like endless adventures.
Slam books filled with secrets and doodles,
Long talks about first crushes, love letters never sent.
When being on Facebook was the peak of cool,
And *"I Belong with You"* played on repeat.
The little shop across the street—
A world within itself, a memory untouched by time.
I remember it all.
And when we sit and reminisce, the years fade away,
For in those moments, we were the happiest,
And maybe, in memory, we still are.

15. Home?

The Thing Is
I can move on...
But I miss the way it felt.
I miss the warmth in the quiet,
The comfort of familiar silence in the morning.
I miss the laughter that used to echo,
The way shadows felt safe at night—
How I used to reach out,
And believe something would be there.
I miss the way stories sounded,
The ritual of six o'clock, every single day.
I miss the sky when it turned soft and stupidly beautiful,
The hush in a half-awake voice.
The thing is,
I can move on...
But sometimes it feels like I lost my anchor.
And maybe we're not meant to lose anchors.
Maybe it had a smile.
Maybe it had a vampire grin.
Maybe it was never mine to keep.

But still...

Have I really lost it?

16. Footprints in Pine and Light

The solo black bird by the waterfall,
Two baby monkeys chasing each other like the world
was theirs,
Tiny wildflowers growing wild on the trail,
Pine cones—chocolate brown and endless, scattered like
forgotten thoughts.
The girl who came for adventure,
But ended up fighting with her boyfriend instead.
A quiet café, waterfall always in the background,
The big golden dog we fed too many chocolate biscuits—
Wouldn't even look at the Maggi.
The little kid, maybe three,
Laughing at everything we said like it was the funniest
thing ever.
A warm common room,
A strange mix of Mongolian rugs and a Middle Eastern
traveler who felt like a story.
The sky full of stars,
Mountains covered in snow,

Just standing there,
Not saying a word.
Instant coffee at the top.
Our hearts racing,
But everything felt still.
Old Bollywood songs playing softly,
The car ride through pitch dark hills.
The furry friend who showed us the way that night—
Miss you.
The strangers who felt like old friends,
The German bakery we didn't go to,
But added to the next time list.
It was all peace,
All joy,
All of it.

17. Whimsy with a straight face

Have you seen colors stolen from a rainbow?
Have you seen trees tickling the clouds?
Have you seen stars twinkling with all the gossip?
Have you seen waterfalls making noise like a class of
naughty kids?
Have you seen spiders always under pressure,
as if trying to live up to the stories we created?
Have you seen fruits getting tired of flying yoga, falling
down?
Do you think caterpillars have beauty salons in their
cocoons?
Or is there a secret shop where flowers buy their
perfume?
If there is, I think it would work like a lottery—
like Bertie Bott's Every Flavour Beans.
Do they also have their own fashion designers?
It must be stressful to create a perfect dress that exists a
lifetime.
Why do you think we're so afraid of lizards?

Is it because they resemble miniature dinosaurs and
dragons?
Have you seen fireflies?
Do they collect their light like pixies?
Do our guardian angels rip their hair out
watching our life choices?
Do ghosts sit with popcorn to watch us?
Why are ants such sweet tooths?
It's unfair their mums don't scold them!
Is it true rabbits live underground
because they're ashamed and other animals tease them?
Do butterflies compete on beauty,
or do they gracefully accept that beauty is in diversity?
Have you seen snakes crawl?
Do you think they ever wish to fly?
Do you think giraffes get bullied for their tall necks?
Do you think penguins go on a keto diet?
I guess we will never know.
Maybe the world keeps its secrets
so we keep asking questions.
Maybe the questions matter more than the answers.
Maybe that's how the magic stays alive.

18. Before I Knew it was Beautiful

Can I go back... just twenty years?
I want to fall sick again,
so Mum can cuddle me the whole day.
I want to race Papa in the park,
pretending the school sports day actually mattered.
I want to sleep at Nani's house,
where dreams felt softer, and the world, kinder.
I want to keep that quiet ritual—
fried snacks with Nanu, every evening without fail.
I want bedtime stories again,
told night after night, like prayers.
I want to go on school picnics,
run wild, spill juice, and feel endless.
I want to play hide and seek until the streetlights blinked
on,
and nothing else existed.
I want to sit beside my parents,
watching daily soaps on Doordarshan like it was a
sacred routine.

I want my parents to be proud of me again,
the way their eyes used to light up—unfiltered,
unquestioning.
I want to be the only child again,
when the whole world felt like it belonged to me.
I want to wake up excited for the day,
even if nothing big was waiting.
I want to throw tantrums
so my chocolate bar could "walk" with me to school.
I want to make silly demands from Daadu,
just to hear his playful sigh before saying yes.
I want to play till the sun disappeared,
and time didn't matter.
I want to collect hairclips again—
little, sparkly pieces of joy.
I want to wear whatever I liked,
without being told I'm too old, too childish.
I want to be called "the best child" again,
and believe it without doubt.
I want to see that same old faith in their eyes,
the kind that made me believe I could do anything.
I want to hand over the reins of life to Papa again,
and just watch the beautiful moments unfold.
Because some days,
when adulting feels too heavy,
I just wish—
I could go back once.

Back to the peace and love I didn't know I was
swimming in.

37

19. Hope with Scraped Knees

I saw the starry sky, wonderstruck,
And thought—am I made of stardust?
Do I also carry the same light?
Do I also shine for others?
Am I the only person who is not able to realise her
worth?
Or am I just a flicker in this universe?
But then, I saw a wildflower grow through a crack in the
stone,
And wondered—
Am I a wildflower too?
Do I contribute to keeping the trust that life finds its
way?
Soft, stubborn,
Still blooming where I was never meant to grow?
Then I saw the beautiful sky,
Changing and shifting,
So transparent,
Cries when it is overwhelmed,

Dresses in pink and blue like a Barbie—without the fear
of judgment from others,
Thundering when people cross their limits—so strong,
Sometimes wears a weary white fluffy dress like an
angel,
Or is simple and graceful other times.
I heard a waterfall crash down the side of a silent
mountain,
Loud and alive,
And it made me wonder—
Am I a waterfall too?
Tumbling, fighting for its path?
Do I have that patience?
Am I a fighter too?
Do I also have a dream like her—to reach the sea?
Do I also have hope?
Why is hope considered something soft and covered in
sunshine?
To me, it's a stubborn child with scraped knees and
elbows,
Yet smiling, playing through all of it.
Can I please be that?
Maybe I am all of it—
A little bit sky,
A little bit wildflower,
A little bit storm and stardust and messy grace.
I hope I wasn't meant to be just one thing.

I hope I am meant to feel everything.

20. Echoes of an 85-Year Life

Sometimes, I just sit and watch him—
his silence louder than most voices,
his presence like old songs you don't play often
but remember every word of.
My grandfather is 85.
I look at his hands—
weathered like the branches of a wise old tree.
I've heard him tell the same stories
over and over again—
yet somehow, they still pull me in
like I'm hearing them for the first time.
He remembers my childhood better than I do.
He rarely says he's proud of me—
and sometimes I wonder,
am I not enough?
But when he does...
it feels like I'm holding the whole world in my hands.
He tells tales of a world I'll never touch.
hard to picture him as a 7-year-old boy,
running barefoot to school,

living through the echo of Gandhi being shot,
watching his hometown bloom from dirt paths
to concrete chaos.
Still—
after all this time,
he is so unbelievably pure.
We joke about how simple he is
in this clever, cunning world.
But honestly?
Maybe we're the fools.
He wears his legacy
in the folds of his skin,
in the lines that whisper every year he's lived.
He worries, sometimes too much,
that his bloodline should remain prestigious.
But why?
Doesn't he trust the world he raised us in?
Doesn't he trust *me*?
Does he ever see a piece of himself in me?
Even a sliver?
Maybe in the way I hoard books
like they hold the answers
he never had time to look for.
I wonder—
does he have unfinished dreams
that don't involve anyone else?
And if he does...

can I carry a piece of them forward?
Just a little?

43

21. Fluffy Clouds

I like clouds.
I like how they drift, shift, and fade,
never asking to be noticed, yet always there.
I like the sunset-orange, yellow-kissed clouds—
they make me nostalgic.
I like the deep purple-blue-white ones—
their beauty leaves me in awe.
I like the sky-blue, almost plain clouds,
with that rare white streak stretching across—
they make me feel at home.
I like the baby-pink clouds,
sprinkled with yellow against a soft blue sky—
they give me Barbie feelings.
I like the sunrise clouds,
burning almost blood-red—
somehow, they bring me peace.
But my favorite?
The fluffy ones—
floating endlessly on a light blue canvas,
like infinite cotton candy.

They heal my inner child.

45